MW00875257

A CHILDREN'S BOOK TO LEARN

NIGERIA

BY JOSEPHINE GRANT

Copyright © 2024 by Josephine Grant

All rights reserved. No part of this book may be reproduced, stored in a retrieval system, or transmitted in any form or by any means—electronic, mechanical, photocopying, recording, or otherwise—without the prior written permission of the publisher, except in the case of brief quotations embodied in critical articles and reviews.

Published and designed by Josephine Grant
ISBN: 9798329249019

For permissions and other inquiries, contact: josephinegrant89@gmail.com

First Edition: 2024

Printed in United Kingdom

CONTENTS

THE COUNTRY

CULTURE

EVERYDAY LIFE

A WARM WELCOME......

HELLO, EXPLORERS!

MY NAME IS JOSEPHINE GRANT, AND JUST LIKE YOU, I LOVE TO LEARN ABOUT THE WORLD AROUND US. I'M THRILLED TO HAVE YOU JOIN ME ON THIS AMAZING JOURNEY THROUGH NIGERIA!

IN THIS BOOK, YOU WILL DISCOVER FASCINATING FACTS ABOUT NIGERIA, FROM ITS VIBRANT CITIES TO ITS LUSH LANDSCAPES. YOU'LL LEARN ABOUT THE POPULATION, THE DIVERSE CLIMATE, AND THE UNIQUE CUSTOMS THAT MAKE NIGERIA SO SPECIAL. WE'LL EXPLORE THE MUSIC THAT FILLS THE AIR AND EVEN SOME POPULAR SAYINGS THAT YOU MIGHT HEAR ON THE STREETS OF LAGOS.

I HOPE YOU ENJOY EVERY MOMENT OF THIS BOOK.

P.S. KEEP YOUR EYES OPEN FOR THE NEXT BOOK IN THE SERIES—WHO KNOWS WHERE WE'LL GO NEXT!

THE COUNTRY.....

Nigeria is located on the western coast of Africa. It is bordered by the Atlantic Ocean to the south, Benin to the west, Niger to the north, and Chad and Cameroon to the east.

Nigeria is the most populous English-speaking country in Africa, making it a unique blend of diverse ethnic cultures and traditions.

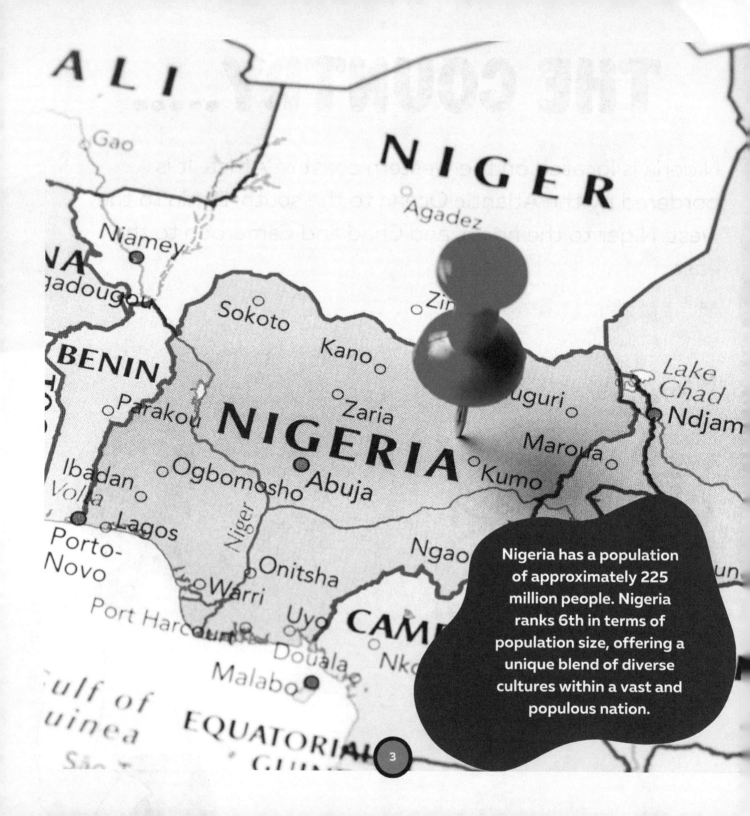

Nigeria has a population of approximately 225 million people. Nigeria ranks 6th in terms of population size, offering a unique blend of diverse cultures within a vast and populous nation.

MORE ABOUT THE COUNTRY......

Nigeria has an amazing and diverse landscape. You can explore thick rainforests, vast savannas, and beautiful rivers all across the country. Some of its most famous natural wonders include the impressive Zuma Rock, the mighty Niger River, and the scenic Jos Plateau. Other cool places to visit are the green and wild Yankari National Park, the stunning Olumo Rock, and the peaceful Obudu Mountain Resort. With tons of exotic animals and gorgeous plants, Nigeria is a true paradise.

5

IKOYI BRIDGE

LOCATION, LOCATION, LOCATION......

Nigeria is in Africa, the second largest and second most populated continent in the world. Nigeria is often called the "Giant of Africa" because it has a huge population and a strong economy. The country shares a lot of cultural similarities with other West African nations, including Benin, Burkina Faso, Cape Verde, Côte d'Ivoire, The Gambia, Ghana, Guinea, Guinea-Bissau, Liberia, Mali, Niger, Senegal, Sierra Leone, and Togo. Nigeria plays a big role in the region and has strong connections with these neighboring countries.

BIG IMPACT......

Nigeria covers about 356,669 square miles (923,769 square kilometers), making it the 14th largest country in Africa and the 32nd largest country in the world. It's the most populous country in Africa, with diverse landscapes and vibrant ecosystems that make it a land of incredible beauty and adventure.

MEMORABLE CITIES......

Nigeria has many cities and towns, each with its own special feel. The capital city, Abuja, is in the center of the country and is where the government is based. Lagos, the biggest city, is a busy place known for its lively culture and important role in the economy. Other key cities include Kano, famous for its rich history and business; Ibadan, known for its schools and universities; and Port Harcourt, which is important for Nigeria's oil industry.

DID YOU KNOW?

ZUMA ROCK IS NOTABLE FOR ITS STRIKING APPEARANCE, WHICH IS SAID TO RESEMBLE A HUMAN FACE.

THE CAPITAL.....

Abuja, the lively capital city of Nigeria, is located right in the center of the country. It covers about 713 square miles and serves as the political and administrative heart of Nigeria. The city has several well-known districts and neighborhoods, like Asokoro, Maitama, Wuse, and Garki, each with its own unique style. Abuja is home to important government buildings, including the Presidential Complex, National Assembly, and Supreme Court. It also has major cultural landmarks, such as the Nigerian National Mosque and the Nigerian National Christian Centre.

THE STATES OF NIGERIA.....

Nigeria is divided into 36 states and one Federal Capital Territory, each with its own unique identity and natural beauty. These states include places like Lagos, Kano, Rivers, Anambra, Ogun, Oyo, Kaduna, Enugu, Benue, Borno, Delta, Ebonyi, Edo, Ekiti, Gombe, Imo, Jigawa, Kebbi, Kogi, Kwara, Nasarawa, Niger, Ondo, Osun, Plateau, Sokoto, Taraba, Yobe, Zamfara, and many more. The Federal Capital Territory is where Abuja, the nation's capital, is located.

Abuja's population is around 3.6 million residents, making it one of the most important urban centers in Nigeria.

ABUJA CENTRAL MOSQUE

LET'S LOOK A LITTLE CLOSER

Lagos State is known for its busy city life and lively culture. Kano State is famous for its rich history and strong trade. Rivers State is well-known for its oil-rich lands and waterways. In the northern regions, like Borno and Sokoto, you'll find beautiful landscapes with savannas and historical sites, as well as a lot of cultural heritage. The southeastern regions, like Enugu and Ebonyi, have green hills and important mineral resources, adding to Nigeria's diverse and beautiful scenery.

AND THE TOWNS....

Nigeria is home to many towns, each with its own special charm and character, adding to the country's rich cultural landscape. Ibadan, in Oyo State, is known for its schools and historical importance, offering a look into Nigeria's academic and cultural heritage. Abeokuta, one of Nigeria's oldest towns, is famous for its beautiful colonial buildings and has a rich history in the cocoa and palm oil industries. Jos, often called the "Home of Peace and Tourism," is a busy center for tin mining and ecotourism, located on the scenic Jos Plateau. Onitsha, along the Niger River in Anambra State, is a lively commercial town known for its bustling markets and trade. Each of these towns, with their unique histories and local cultures, plays an important role in Nigeria's social and economic life.

RAINY, DRY AND ALOT OF SUNSHINE...

Nigeria has a diverse climate with both tropical and arid weather patterns. In the southern regions, the climate is tropical, with hot and humid weather all year round. In the northern regions, the climate is more arid, meaning it's very dry with little rainfall and much hotter conditions. Nigeria has two main seasons: the rainy season, which usually lasts from April to October, and the dry season, which runs from November to March.

IT'S A WALK IN A PARK......

Nigeria has many parks and protected areas that show off its beautiful nature and rich wildlife. Yankari Game Reserve is a large wildlife reserve focused on conservation and eco-tourism, where you can see animals like elephants, lions, and various birds. Cross River National Park is famous for its lush rainforests and is home to rare primates like the Cross River gorilla. Gashaka Gumti National Park, the largest in Nigeria, has a mix of landscapes, from savannas to mountain forests, making it a great spot for people who love wildlife.

15

MILLENNIUM PARK, ABUJA

GREEN WHITE GREEN

The flag of Nigeria is called the "Green-White-Green." It has three vertical stripes: green on the left and right, and white in the middle. The green stripes show Nigeria's rich land and farming, symbolizing growth and wealth. The white stripe stands for peace and unity, representing the country's hopes for harmony. This flag represents Nigeria's natural resources, its wish for peace, and its strong spirit.

16

UNITY AND FAITH, PEACE AND PROGRESS

NIGERIA FLAG

17

COOL AS A EAGLE

Nigeria's national animal is the eagle, a symbol of strength, power, and vision. The eagle is shown on Nigeria's coat of arms and is an important symbol for the country. It represents the hopes of the nation, the strong spirit of its people, and the country's rich natural heritage. The eagle stands for resilience, courage, and determination, reflecting Nigeria's strong spirit and its drive for greatness.

The African Fish Eagle is commonly found near large bodies of water such as rivers and lakes, where it hunts for fish with its powerful talons.

The lyrics to the Nigerian National Anthem are:

"Arise, O Compatriots"
Arise, O compatriots,
Nigeria's call obey
To serve our fatherland
With love and strength and faith.
The labor of our heroes past
Shall never be in vain,
To serve with heart and might
One nation bound in freedom, peace, and unity.

THE TASTIEST DISH

Jollof rice is Nigeria's national dish. It's a colourful and tasty meal made with rice, tomatoes, onions, and spices. Sometimes, chicken, fish, or beef is added, and it's often topped with vegetables. Jollof rice is popular at parties and gatherings, showing Nigeria's rich food culture. This dish is loved by people all over the country and brings families and friends together.

JOURNEY THROUGH TIME....

Nigeria has a long history that goes back thousands of years. The region was first home to indigenous peoples like the Nok, Ife, and Benin civilisations, who left behind a rich legacy of art and culture. In the late 19th century, the British began colonising the area. Nigeria gained independence from Britain on 1 October 1960, starting its modern era.

NOK

IFE

NIGERIA'S EVOLUTION.....

The people of Nigeria come from a mix of different cultures. The first inhabitants were various ethnic groups like the Yoruba, Hausa, Igbo, and Fulani, each with their own unique traditions and customs. Later, the transatlantic slave trade and British colonisation introduced new influences and interactions among these groups.

After gaining independence, Nigeria continued to grow as a nation of diverse ethnicities, languages, and religions.

VIBRANT STYLES....

Fashion in Nigeria has changed a lot over the years, influenced by the different cultures within the country. Traditional clothing includes the Yoruba agbada and buba, the Hausa babanriga and kaftan, and the Igbo isiagu and wrapper. Nigerian fashion also features vibrant lace fabrics and intricate beadwork, showing the rich cultural heritage of its diverse ethnic groups.

25

FASHION TODAY?....

Today, Nigerian fashion is a mix of traditional and modern styles, often seen at cultural celebrations and festivals. Designers blend old and new elements to create unique and stylish outfits, like the elegant agbada or the chic iro and buba. Nigerian fashion reflects the country's rich culture and creativity. Events like Lagos Fashion Week celebrate the beauty and variety of Nigerian clothing. Famous fashion icons like Agbani Darego, who was the first Nigerian to win Miss World, have captured audiences with their style and grace, further showcasing the richness of Nigerian fashion.

POLITICS

Nigeria's political history has been shaped by many important leaders since independence. Nnamdi Azikiwe, the first President, helped Nigeria become independent. Sir Abubakar Tafawa Balewa, the first Prime Minister, set up Nigeria's parliamentary democracy. General Yakubu Gowon led the country through the civil war and worked to keep it united. More recent leaders, like Olusegun Obasanjo and Muhammadu Buhari, have continued to shape the country's policies. Each leader has helped Nigeria grow and modernise in different ways.

Nnamdi Azikiwe

Obafemi Awolowo

ABOUT THE PRESIDENTS.....

Nnamdi Azikiwe (1963-1966)

Nnamdi Azikiwe, often referred to as "Zik," was Nigeria's first President and a key figure in the country's struggle for independence. He played a pivotal role in promoting national unity and advocating for self-governance.

Olusegun Obasanjo (1976-1979, 1999-2007)

Olusegun Obasanjo is a prominent figure in Nigerian politics, having served as both a military head of state and a civilian president. His first tenure (1976-1979) focused on the transition to civilian rule, while his second tenure (1999-2007) was marked by economic reforms and efforts to combat corruption.

ABOUT THE PRESIDENTS....

Muhammadu Buhari (1983-1985, 2015-2023)

Muhammadu Buhari has had a significant impact on Nigeria's political landscape, serving as both a military ruler and a civilian president. His military regime (1983-1985) focused on fighting corruption and indiscipline.

Goodluck Jonathan (2010-2015)

Goodluck Jonathan served as Nigeria's President from 2010 to 2015, following the death of President Umaru Musa Yar'Adua. Jonathan's presidency was notable for its focus on electoral reforms, economic growth, and improving education. His administration also faced significant challenges, including security issues related to Boko Haram insurgency.

LAND OF LANGUAGES...

The main language in Nigeria is English, which is used in government, schools, and media. Nigeria also has over 500 local languages, with Hausa, Yoruba, and Igbo being the most common. These languages are used in everyday life and cultural events. Nigerian Pidgin, a mix of English and local languages, is also widely spoken, especially in informal settings. This shows Nigeria's rich culture and how it keeps traditional languages alive alongside English.

EXPLORE HAUSA....

Hausa is a major language traditionally spoken by the people of northern Nigeria. It is characterized by its unique pronunciation, extensive vocabulary, and complex grammar, reflecting the rich cultural heritage and diverse influences of the Hausa people.

Hausa serves not only as a mother tongue for many but also as a lingua franca across much of West Africa, facilitating communication and trade among different ethnic groups.

31

EXPLORE YORUBA...

Some key features of Yoruba include:

Tonal Language: Yoruba is a tonal language with three primary tones: high, mid, and low. The meaning of words can change based on the tone used.

Nasal Sounds: Nasal vowels are common, where the air passes through the nose while pronouncing the vowel (e.g., "ẹ" as in "ẹbọ").

Consonant Sounds: Some consonants in Yoruba have unique sounds not found in English, such as "gb" and "kp."

Syllable Structure: Words typically have an open syllable structure, often ending in vowels rather than consonants (e.g., "baba" for father).

Pronunciation Variations: Pronunciation can vary by region, with slight differences in how certain vowels and consonants are articulated.

EXPLORE IGBO.....

Igbo includes many unique words and expressions, such as "kedụ" (how are you), "nara" (take), and "nwata" (child).

Tonal Variations: Igbo is a tonal language, and tones can affect the meaning of words significantly.

Pronouns and Prefixes: Pronouns and verb prefixes are used extensively to indicate tense, mood, and aspect. For example, "m ga" means "I will," and "o na" means "he/she is.

Simplified Grammar: Compared to Standard English, Igbo grammar can be more streamlined, with fewer verb conjugations and more straightforward sentence structures.

Double Negatives: Double negatives are sometimes used for emphasis, similar to some informal English dialects.

DIVERSITY OF NIGERIA...

Nigeria is a vibrant and multiethnic country, shaped by centuries of diverse ethnic groups and cultural exchange. The country is home to over 250 ethnic groups and numerous tribes, each with its own unique traditions and customs.

The country's multiculturalism is celebrated through events like the Eyo Festival in Lagos, the Durbar Festival in Kano, and the Osun-Osogbo Festival in Osun State.

MAKES ME WANT TO DANCE..

Nigerian music is a lively mix of rhythms and styles, showing the country's diverse culture. Traditional music like Highlife and Fuji tells stories of everyday life and cultural practices. Afrobeat, created by Fela Kuti, mixes African rhythms with jazz and funk, and is known for its energetic beats and social messages. Juju music, rooted in Yoruba culture, has lively guitar riffs and percussion. Modern genres like Afrobeats, hip-hop, and gospel are also popular, making Nigerian music vibrant and ever-changing. Nigeria's music continues to inspire artists around the world.

37

NIGERIAN MUSIC CONTINUED.....

Nigeria has produced many talented musicians who have made a big impact on the world of music. Fela Kuti, the pioneer of Afrobeat, mixed African rhythms with jazz and funk to create a lively and socially conscious genre. King Sunny Adé is a major figure in Juju music, bringing Yoruba sounds to the world with his lively guitar riffs and percussion. Burna Boy, a modern Afrobeats artist, is known globally for his unique mix of Afrobeat, reggae, and dancehall. These artists, and many others, showcase Nigeria's rich musical heritage and its influence on music around the world.

NIGERIAN HITMAKERS.........

Here are some renowned Nigerian musicians who have made significant contributions to the world of music.

FELA KUTI

Known as the pioneer of Afrobeat, Fela Kuti blended African rhythms with jazz and funk influences, creating music that was both energetic and socially conscious, often addressing political and social issues in Nigeria.

KING SUNNY ADÉ

A leading figure in Juju music, King Sunny Adé brought Yoruba sounds to international audiences with his lively guitar riffs and intricate percussion.

BURNA BOY

A modern Afrobeats superstar, Burna Boy has gained global recognition with his unique blend of Afrobeat, reggae, and dancehall, winning a Grammy Award and captivating audiences worldwide.

A LANDMARK OR TWO.....

Nigeria is home to many famous landmarks that show its natural beauty and historical importance. Zuma Rock, near Abuja, is a huge monolith known as the "Gateway to Abuja," symbolizing the nation's strength. Aso Rock, also in Abuja, is a large outcrop that is central to the city and houses important government buildings. Olumo Rock in Abeokuta is a historic site that served as a refuge during inter-tribal wars. Other landmarks, like the Osun-Osogbo Sacred Grove, a UNESCO World Heritage site, highlight Nigeria's effort to preserve its unique cultural and natural heritage.

OLUMO ROCK

MORE LANDMARKS.....

Nigeria has stunning architecture and important landmarks. The National Arts Theatre in Lagos, built in the 1970s, is a key cultural center and a great example of modern design. The National Mosque in Abuja, with its big domes and minarets, shows the country's Islamic heritage. The 1999 Constitution of Nigeria Monument in Abuja stands for the country's commitment to democracy. The Nok Terracotta Sculptures, found in central Nigeria, offer a glimpse into one of Africa's oldest and most advanced ancient civilizations.

43

THE NATIONAL
MOSQUE IN ABUJA

A CULINARY EXPERIENCE.....

Nigerian food is a mix of traditional and modern flavours. It has developed over a long time, showing the country's rich history and many cultures. Traditional Nigerian dishes are hearty and full of flavour, often made with local ingredients. Nigerian food is known for its strong spices, unique textures, and the way people enjoy meals together, making every meal special.

MORE FOOD.....

One of the most loved Nigerian dishes is jollof rice, a colourful one-pot meal made with rice, tomatoes, onions, and spices, often served at special occasions and family gatherings. Egusi soup, a thick and savoury dish made with ground melon seeds, leafy vegetables, and various meats or fish, is another staple in Nigerian cooking. Suya, spicy grilled meat on skewers, is a popular street food enjoyed by many. These dishes show the rich culinary heritage and diverse cultural influences of Nigeria.

EGUSI

SUYA

MOI MOI

AKARA

NATION OF SPORT..

Sports are an important part of Nigerian culture, bringing people together through a shared love of competition and teamwork. From busy cities to quiet villages, people of all ages enjoy sports. Nigeria has a proud sporting history with many different sports and events.

Football is the most popular sport, with a passionate fan base and a rich tradition going back to colonial times. The Nigerian national team, the Super Eagles, has had international success, and local leagues attract excited crowds.

WE LOVE FOOTBALL!...

Football is the most popular sport in Nigeria and holds a special place in the hearts of the people. With a history going back to colonial times, football is more than just a game in Nigeria; it's a unifying force that brings people together from all backgrounds. The national team, the Super Eagles, has produced legendary players like Jay-Jay Okocha and Nwankwo Kanu, who have made a big impact on the sport internationally. Local football matches, whether in busy cities or quiet villages, draw passionate crowds and create a lively atmosphere. Venues like the National Stadium in Abuja host exciting international and domestic matches, showing football's importance as a beloved national pastime. The sport's deep roots in Nigerian culture show its lasting appeal and the pride it brings to the people.

A HOME OF AWESOME PLAYERS

JAY-JAY OKOCHA

Augustine Azuka "Jay-Jay" Okocha, a former Nigerian professional footballer, played as an attacking midfielder. During his time with the Nigeria national team from 1993 to 2006, he accumulated 73 caps and scored 14 goals. Furthermore, he was part of three FIFA World Cup squads.

SEGUN ODEGBAMI

Giannis Sina Ugo Antetokounmpo, a professional basketball player for the Milwaukee Bucks in the National Basketball Association, hails from both Greek and Nigerian descent. Due to his remarkable attributes in size, speed, strength, and unique background, he is famously known as the "Greek Freak".

GIANNIS ANTETOKOUNMPO

Patrick Olusegun Odegbami, commonly known as Segun Odegbami, is a former Nigerian professional footballer recognized for his role as a forward.

ATHLETICS......

Athletics is a growing sport in Nigeria, becoming more popular among both athletes and fans. The sport is steadily increasing in the country, with local clubs and schools helping to train a new generation of talent. The Athletics Federation of Nigeria (AFN) plays an important role in promoting the sport by organising tournaments and training programs to build skills and teamwork. Nigeria's national athletics team has done well on the international stage, competing in events like the Olympics and World Championships. Nigerian athletes, like Blessing Okagbare and Tobi Amusan, have won many medals, showing the country's strength in sprinting, long-distance running, and field events.

CUSTOMS

Nigerian customs are a mix of traditions that show the country's diverse culture. Celebrations like Independence Day on 1st October are full of music, dance, and colourful costumes, reflecting the nation's unity and joy.

Family gatherings are a big part of Nigerian life, with meals that showcase the different flavours of Nigerian food. Traditional crafts, storytelling, and folklore are also important in keeping the culture of Nigeria's many ethnic groups alive.

CUSTOMS

Respect for elders, community support, and hospitality are key parts of Nigerian society, making it a welcoming and culturally rich country. These traditions show how Nigeria blends old customs with modern life.

LET'S CELEBRATE!

Celebrations in Nigeria are lively and diverse, showing the country's rich culture. Christmas is widely celebrated with festive decorations, caroling, and traditional meals shared with family and friends. The New Yam Festival, celebrated by the Igbo people, marks the end of the harvest with feasting, dancing, and thanksgiving. Eid al-Fitr and Eid al-Adha are important Muslim holidays, celebrated with prayers, feasts, and giving to charity. These celebrations, and others, show Nigeria's unity in diversity, bringing people together to honour their shared heritage and traditions.

..MORE CELEBRATIONS

Besides major holidays, Nigeria has many other celebrations that show its cultural diversity and community spirit. Emancipation Day, celebrated on 1st August, marks the end of slavery with cultural performances, traditional African drumming, and storytelling. The Argungu Fishing Festival in Kebbi State is a lively event with fishing competitions, cultural displays, and traditional music and dance, celebrating local fishing culture. Easter is celebrated with church services, feasting, and family gatherings, symbolizing the resurrection of Christ. The Igbo people celebrate the New Yam Festival to mark the harvest season with feasting, dancing, and thanksgiving. The Calabar Carnival, called "Africa's Biggest Street Party," happens every December in Cross River State.

WILDLIFE...

Nigeria has a rich and diverse wildlife, thanks to its different ecosystems like savannas, rainforests, and wetlands. The country is home to many animals, including Leopards, Lions, Jackals, Hyenas, Elephants, Manatees, Hippos, Aardvarks, Monkeys, Baboons, Bats, Rats, Mice, and Squirrels, among others. Birdwatchers can enjoy spotting over 900 bird species, like the colorful African grey parrot and the red-cheeked cordon-bleu. Nigeria works to protect its wildlife through national parks and reserves, like Yankari National Park and Gashaka Gumti National Park, helping to preserve its rich biodiversity.

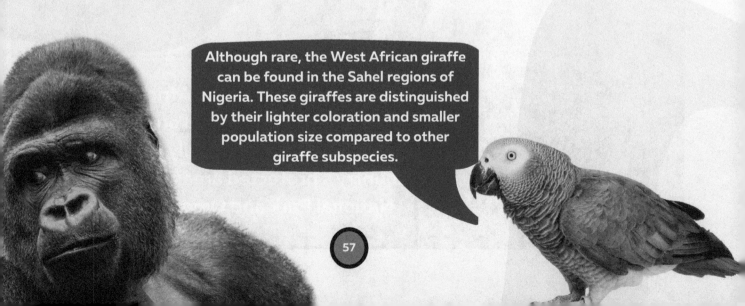

Although rare, the West African giraffe can be found in the Sahel regions of Nigeria. These giraffes are distinguished by their lighter coloration and smaller population size compared to other giraffe subspecies.

Nigeria is home to the African elephant, the largest land animal on Earth. These elephants are primarily found in the country's protected areas, such as Yankari National Park and Omo Forest Reserve.

RED-CHEEKED CORDON-BLEU

BUS...

Buses are a key part of Nigeria's public transportation, used by millions every day. There are different types, like the big BRT buses in Lagos, run by the government, and smaller danfos and mini-buses, which are privately run and found in both cities and rural areas. Despite issues like overcrowding and irregular schedules, buses remain a cheap and easy option for many Nigerians. There are also efforts to improve the bus system to make it more organized, efficient, and safe for passengers.

OKADAS......

Okadas, or motorbike taxis, are an important part of Nigeria's transportation system, especially in busy cities like Lagos, Abuja, and Port Harcourt. They offer a quick and affordable way to get around crowded streets, making them popular with both locals and visitors. Okadas are known for their ability to weave through traffic, providing a fast alternative to cars and buses. However, there are safety concerns, leading some cities to introduce rules to make them safer for riders and passengers. Okada riders are a diverse group, and many rely on this job as their main source of income.

EDUCATION IS IMPORTANT....

Education is very important in Nigeria. There are public and private schools, and the government provides free primary and secondary education. They are trying to improve schools, especially in rural areas. Students learn subjects like maths, science, English, and social studies, and some schools offer technical training. Nigeria also has universities, like the University of Lagos and the University of Ibadan, where students can study further. Even with some challenges, Nigeria is working hard to improve education and help more people learn.

GLOSSARY

Abuja
The capital city of Nigeria, located in the center of the country.

Afrobeat
A music genre that combines African rhythms with jazz, funk, and highlife, pioneered by Fela Kuti.

Aso Rock
A large rock outcrop in Abuja, which houses the Nigerian Presidential Complex, Nigerian National Assembly, and Nigerian Supreme Court.

Benin Kingdom
An ancient African kingdom located in what is now southern Nigeria, known for its advanced art and culture.

Dambe
A traditional form of boxing practiced by the Hausa people of Nigeria, often performed during festivals.

Kano
A major city in northern Nigeria, known for its historical significance and bustling markets.

GLOSSARY

Okada

Motorbike taxis commonly used for transportation in Nigerian cities, known for their ability to navigate traffic quickly.

Pounded Yam

A smooth, stretchy dough made from boiled yam, typically served with soups and stews.

Suya

Spicy skewered meat grilled to perfection, popular as a street food in Nigeria.

Super Eagles

The nickname for the Nigerian national football team.

Yankari National Park

A wildlife park located in Bauch State, known for its hot springs and diverse animal species.

Yoruba

An ethnic group in southwestern Nigeria, known for their vibrant culture and traditions.

A WORD FROM THE AUTHOR

Dear Explorers,

Thank you so much for joining me on this incredible journey through Nigeria! I hope you had as much fun reading and learning about this amazing country as I did writing about it. Remember, the world is full of wonderful places and fascinating stories just waiting to be discovered. Keep your curiosity alive and never stop exploring!

If you enjoyed this book, I would be thrilled if you could leave a positive review on Amazon. Your feedback helps other young adventurers find their way to exciting new destinations.

Happy travels and happy reading!

Warmest wishes,
Josephine Grant

BIBLIOGRAPHY

Books:
1. Falola, Toyin, and Matthew M. Heaton. A History of Nigeria. Cambridge University Press, 2008.
2. Shillington, Kevin. Encyclopedia of African History. Routledge, 2005.
3. Smith, Daniel Jordan. A Culture of Corruption: Everyday Deception and Popular Discontent in Nigeria. Princeton University Press, 2007.
4. Achebe, Chinua. There Was a Country: A Personal History of Biafra. Penguin Books, 2012.
5. Ekwensi, Cyprian. Jagua Nana. Heinemann Educational Books, 1961.

Journal Articles:
1. Ogundele, S.O. "Culture and Customs of the Yoruba." Journal of African Cultural Studies, vol. 16, no. 2, 2004, pp. 125-137.
2. Ajayi, J.F. Ade. "Colonialism: An Episode in African History." Journal of the Historical Society of Nigeria, vol. 2, no. 2, 1961, pp. 195-210.

Websites:
1. Central Bank of Nigeria. "History of Nigerian Currency." Central Bank of Nigeria, www.cbn.gov.ng/Currency/historycur.asp. Accessed 15 June 2024.
2. Nigeria National Parks Service. "Yankari National Park." www.nigeriaparkservice.org/yankari. Accessed 12 June 2024.
3. The British Museum. "Nok Terracottas." The British Museum, www.britishmuseum.org/collection/term/x30694. Accessed 10 June 2024.

BIBLIOGRAPHY

Reports:

- National Bureau of Statistics. Nigeria Demographic and Health Survey 2018. National Population Commission, 2019.
- World Bank. Nigeria Economic Report. World Bank, 2021.

Theses and Dissertations:

- Adedoyin, Oluwakemi. "The Impact of Traditional Music on Contemporary Nigerian Music." PhD diss., University of Lagos, 2015.

Encyclopedia Entries:

- "Nigeria." Encyclopaedia Britannica, Encyclopaedia Britannica, Inc., 2024. www.britannica.com/place/Nigeria.

Made in the USA
Las Vegas, NV
03 October 2024

96225189R00044